Fun Christmas Riddles & Trick Questions For Kids and Family

Stocking Stuffer Edition:
300 Riddles and Brain Teasers
That
Kids and Family Will Enjoy!

Riddleland

Christmas Riddles

Christmas Riddles

Table of Contents

Christmas Riddles

Introduction

"Christmas is a day of meaning and traditions, a special day spent in the warm circle of family and friends" ~ Margaret Thatcher

We would like to personally thank you for purchasing this book. **Fun Halloween Riddles and Trick Questions for Kids and Family!** book is a collection of 300 fun brain teasers and riddles of easy to hard difficulty.

These brain teasers will challenge the children and their parents to think and stretch their minds. They have also many other benefits such as:

- **Bonding** – It is an excellent way for parents and their children to spend some quality time and create some fun and memorable memories.

Christmas Riddles

- **Confidence Building** - When parents give the riddles, it creates a safe environment for children to burst out answers even if they are incorrect. This helps the children to develop self confidence in expressing themselves.

- **Improve Vocabulary** – Riddles are usually written in advance words, therefore children will need to understand these words before they can share the riddles.

- **Better reading comprehension** – Many children can read at a young age but may not understand the context of the sentences. Riddles can help develop the children's interest to comprehend the context before they can share it to their friends.

- **Sense of humor** –Funny creative riddles can help children develop their sense of humor while getting their brains working.

Get the Bonus Book!

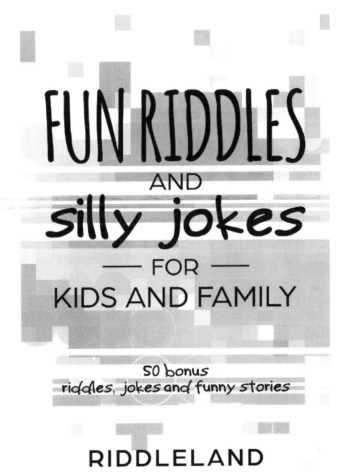

https://bit.ly/riddlelandbonusbook

Thank you for buying this book, We would like to share a special bonus as a token of appreciation. It is collection 50 original jokes, riddles and 2 super funny stories!

RIDDLES AND JOKES CONTESTS!!

Riddleland is having **2 contests** to see who is the smartest or funniest boys and girls in the world!

1) **Creative and Challenging Riddles**
2) **Tickle Your Funny Bone Contest**

Parents, please email us your child's "Original" Riddle or Joke **and he or she could win a $50 gift card to Amazon.**

Here are the rules:

1) It must be challenging for the riddles and funny for the jokes!
2) It must be 100% Original and not something from the internet! It is easy to find out!
3) You can submit both joke and riddle as they are 2 separate contests.
4) No help from the parents unless they are as funny as you.
5) Winners will be announced via email.
6) Email us at Riddleland@riddlelandforkids.com

Chapter 1: Easy Riddles

"Christmas is a necessity. There has to be at least one day of the year to remind us that we're here for something else besides ourselves." ~ Eric Sevareid

1. Cold frost

I am cold and powdery. You build me from the ground up. Don't touch me without gloves on or you will get frostbite. Build me up during the night. But don't get too attached. I will be gone when the sun starts shining. What am I?

2. Standing big and tall

I am around all year long standing big and tall, but because of the cold, my leaves are gone. What am I?

3. Joyous Season

Though it's often gloomy outside, this time of year brings joyous festivities. With the lights, decorations, gifts and cheer. This time of year, it is hard to be sad. What time of year am I?

4. Tall and naked outside

When I am outside, I am tall and naked, just taking in nature. When I am inside, you light me up and decorate me beyond recognition. You love to gather around me on Christmas morning. What am I?

5. Christmas ornaments

Robert buys a fully decorated Christmas tree. The tree is about eight feet tall and three feet wide. About how many ornaments will he need for the tree?

6. Only you hear me out

I am a popular Christmas gift. You can hear me but no one else can. I can cover your whole head, or just sit in your ears. What Am I?

7. Festive song in doorstep

I am a festive song. People want to sing me so much that they will even come to your front door so you can hear me.

8. Crystals from the sky

I fall from the sky like little crystals. You hate me when I get too cold and make you slip and fall down. But you love me when I get school canceled for you. What am I?

9. White fluffy and tasty

I am white, fluffy, tasty and sometimes you put me in your hot chocolate. What am I?

10. Sometimes hung or bitten

I am red and white. Sometimes I am green and yellow or white and blue. I am named after something people use to help them walk. Sometimes you hang me from your Christmas tree, and sometimes you like to take a bite out of me. What am I?

11. Marshmallows in cocoa

Mikey loves to eat sweet things. He bought a cup of hot cocoa with extra marshmallows that are perfect to his taste. He generally likes about 10 small marshmallows in his cocoa for it to be perfect. How many should he add to his drink?

12. Small and pointy ears

I am low to the ground, but I also have pointy ears. Don't mess with me because I also help the big jolly red guy who brings you your gifts. Who am I?

13. Fresh and sweet mint

I have a minty taste, and I melt in your mouth and make it feel fresh and sweet. Despite my name, I am not spicy at all. What am I?

14. The 5th friend

Kally, Kelly, Killy and Kolly are friends who go to the movies on Christmas night. What is the fifth friends name?

15. Hot cocoa stealer

While Jimmy left the room for a few minutes on a cold Christmas night. Someone drank his hot cocoa. Everyone in the house had a story of where they were. Billy was out raking leaves. Tommy was in the other room watching a movie and Eddie was sitting at the counter reading. Who drank the hot cocoa?

16. Shiny red-nosed creature

Flying at night through the thick fog is easy for me, because I am a shining light, in a world of darkness. I move with ease with my shiny red nose, and once others understood this about me, they loved me. Who am I?

17. Magical kissing plant

I may just look like a leaf or plant, but I have some magical powers where when people walk under me, they turn and kiss each other. What am I?

18. Drink from apples

I was born on a tree, filled with apples. When I come to your town, I am tangy and brown. I start off as a solid, but I come to you as a liquid. A delicious one that you can drink. What am I?

19. The smoky way

If you don't have me in your home, then Santa cannot come inside. On Christmas morning, I am essential. Most of the year, I am just full of smoke. What am I?

20. Rip me off

I am decorative, but I am not on your tree. I am actually under your tree. I am part of your gift, but not actually your gift. I am actually a nuisance to you because with me, you cannot tell what your gift is. Until Christmas when you rip me off and reveal what is under me. What am I?

21. Small but edible

I look like something you would live in, but I am small and edible. What am I?

22. Donner's shiny red nose

How far is the distance that Donner can see with his shiny red nose?

23. Slippery when cold

Watch out for me this holiday season. I am slippery, but often invisible to the naked eye. I am on the ground when it is cold. Go over me and you will have a mighty fall. What am I?

24. Wrapped for surprise

I am wrapped in fancy paper, and you don't know what I am. I am big, I am small, I am square, I am round, I am hard, and I am soft. I lay under the Christmas tree, mysterious as ever. Your sole purpose in life becomes finding out what I am until Christmas morning? I am waiting for you under that tree, so what am I?

25. Identified flying object

I fly through the night, but I have no wings. In fact, I am not even a living being. My parking spot is on your rooftop. I provide a comfortable ride for Santa. What am I?

26. Half cookies

Jim has four Christmas tree shaped cookies of the same sizes. He ate half of each cookie and he put the rest in a pan with the half pieces he had left shaped like two cookies. How did he do it?

27. Sleigh velocity

Santa whizzes around during the night going from house to house at the speed of light. If he can come to 10 houses in 0.5 seconds, how fast is the sleigh moving when it is parked on a rooftop?

28. Toy production

I am filled with little people running around, animals that can fly, and a big red jolly guy. I am where your toys are built by many hardworking elves. What am I?

29. Above the fireplace

I hang above your fireplace. You are happy to see me stuffed, but you can't wait to empty me. Whatever gift is, even if too small won't go under the Christmas tree, is instead inside of me. What am I?

30. Flying without wings

I can fly, but I have no wings. I am a living creature and I have magical powers. I am full of antlers, but you will not catch me in the forest. I prefer the extreme cold. I guide Santa on Christmas morning. What am I?

31. **Words along the gift**

You open me on Christmas morning, along with your gifts. My words bring tears to your eyes as I share love for you that came from another person. What am I?

32. **Where's the Christmas tree**

Bob walks 50 feet uphill from his driveway to chop down a Christmas tree. He walks back down 50 feet to his car. The inside of the car is filled with items for Christmas. The roof of the car has his ski equipment attached to it. Where did he place the tree?

33. **Chopped Christmas trees**

Thomas was able to chop down three Christmas trees in about 20 minutes. How long would it take him to chop down the same trees with a chainsaw if he can get it done twice as fast?

34. **Flames for cold nights**

I keep you warm on a cold Christmas night, but I am just located in one place in the house, and I am full of flames. What am I?

35. Glides on ice

Walk on ice, and you'll slip and fall. But, wear these, and you will glide with ease. What are they?

36. Goes inside a sock

I go inside a decorative sock, but I am not your feet. I am a gift, but I do not go under a tree but above your fireplace. What am I?

37. Mesmerizes on your doorstep

I come to your front door full of glee. Answer your door or not, you will be mesmerized by my singing voice. I sing the classics, but I also take request. I go from door to door spreading Christmas cheer.

38. Family Caroling

A family of four go out Christmas Caroling. They all go to their first house, and now four different households felt their Christmas cheer. How did they cover four house on their first stop?

39. Pile of snow

I am a bank, but I do not carry money. I am made from snow, but not a snowman. I am usually just in one big pile. What am I?

40. Night meal

Call me by the wrong name, and it's ok, but don't call me late for this on Christmas night, or I will miss a mighty meal with the family. What will I miss?

41. Suburban house

My friend has a one-story house in the suburbs. He decorated it heavily for Christmas. He decided to stick to a single-color theme. The front door is green, the tree is green, the wreath is green, the stockings are green, the furniture is covered in green, and the carpet is green. What color would he have decorated the stairs?

42. Artificial Christmas Tree

Jimmy wants to get an artificial Christmas tree this year. Should he buy it from a tree lot or cut down a fresh one in the forest?

43. Bulky Christmas tree

Tommy has a large bulky Christmas tree in his living room on the first floor. He wants to take it outside after the holidays. Since it is so large, what is the best way for him to carry it down the stairs, so he does not hurt his back?

44. Magnificent Snowman

Dominic built a snowman in the backyard. It took him hours, and he made it eight feet tall. It was a magnificent structure, indeed. The only thing he's worried about is that his neighbor's dog runs all over the front yard sometimes. What can he do to keep the dog from knocking over the snowman?

45. Eat all you cane

Johnny ate all of his candy canes. He wants to make sure his little brother does not eat the rest. How can he make sure this does not happen?

46. Your wish is my command

James is sitting on his couch, watching TV on Christmas eve. Suddenly, a magical fairy appears and tells him that she will grant him three wishes for Christmas. James gets excited and thinks carefully about all of his wishes. After a couple of minutes, the magical fairy says that she will grant him a fourth wish if his last wish will be to set her free from being a fairy. James says ok and decides to make his first three wishes. He wishes for a family, a car and a new house. The magical fairy gives him what he asks for including the fourth wish. What do you think James' fourth wish will be?

47. Left before they wake up

On Christmas eve, Jim wants to leave for work early before his kids wake up so that he can sneak their gifts under the tree without them knowing. What time should he wake up his kids for breakfast?

48. The fallen Christmas tree

Jane buys two Christmas trees for her house so she can set one up in her living room and one upstairs in her bedroom. The one from upstairs falls down the stairs. How many Christmas trees does she have left?

49. Granny's clock

Billy really needs some advice, so he goes up to his grandfather's clock to ask a few questions. He asks the clock three total questions: Dear Grandfather clock, 1) What should I get my wife for Christmas? 2)Will my kids still love me if I cannot get them expensive gifts? 3) Will I get my Christmas bonus this year? If you were the clock, how should you answer these questions?

50. Candy canes with friends

Billy, Freddy, and Tommy have 10 candy canes. Billy gives one of his to Freddy and Freddy gives two of his to Tommy. Tommy really does not like candy canes, so he gives all of his to Billy. How many candy canes do they have left?

51. Christmas tree star

Mike buys a star to put on top of his Christmas tree in the living room. The tree is 10 feet tall. When he gets home, he puts the bags down and goes into the kitchen to get something to eat. There is nothing near the tree to climb up near the top. When Mike walks back into the living room, he sees his son carrying the star. How did he get it?

52. Christmas first

When you're here, Christmas comes before Halloween and Thanksgiving.

53. Santa knows best

You meet Santa Clause and become excited. You ask him for a few things, and he says to call him in the morning. You get up the next day and call Santa, and he picks up immediately before the first ring is even done and calls you immediately by your name. You ask Santa how he knew it was you calling. What is his reply?

54. Race in boots

Santa wins a five-mile race in boots. What place did he get if he was racing against five really fast reindeer?

55. Santa eats cookies

James only has five cookies to leave out for Santa. On Christmas morning, Santa is eating 10 cookies at James' house. How is this possible?

56. All I want for Christmas

On Christmas Day, how do you say that you want something?

57. Gifts for four

Jane's mom buys a Christmas gift for all four of her daughters. Her first three daughters' names are April, May and June. What is the fourth daughter's name?

58. Santa's special coat

Santa keeps a special coat in his closet that he uses to go out every year the day after Christmas. This year, he promises Mrs. Claus that he will not go out anywhere. During the night, Mrs. Claus opens their closet and realizes Santa was fibbing. How does she know?

59. Cookies for Rudolph

Sammy wants to show his appreciation on Christmas. How many cookies should he leave out for Rudolph on Christmas morning?

60. Decorative ice

I resemble ice, but I am not cold. You will not slip on me but will use me to decorate. I come in small strips and I am shiny and sparkly. You can't put real ice on your indoor Christmas tree, but put me and I will be the next best thing. What am I?

61. Two cousins apart

Jim's two cousins live ten miles apart. He drives 10 miles to see the first cousin on Christmas. After this, he drives 10 miles back to his home. He has now seen both of his cousins. How did he do it?

62. Holiday with Christmas

I am my own holiday, but I am often incorporated with Christmas.

63. Egg Nog glass

It takes Abel three large sips to finish an 8-ounce glass of egg nog. At the party, he makes a bet that he can drink egg nog from an 8-ounce glass in one sip. He pours the drink and in one large sip, finishes it. How did he do it?

64. Plum dessert

Despite the name of this soft dessert, it has no plum in it.

65. Walloping drink

I am a fun and tasty drink containing fruit or fruit juice. I really pack a wallop, but it is with my taste.

66. Where's my punch

Jamie has been drinking her punch, and suddenly her old friend walks up to say hi. She pours some punch too, and then they both set them down on the table and talk. When they look at their glasses, they forgot who put their punch where. How will they figure this out?

67. Beautifies any gift

Often wrapped around outside of a gift for beauty, may also be in front of a new store opening.

68. Decorating the trees

In a large shopping mall, there were three large Christmas trees. Three people were tasked with decorating the trees. Over one weekend, All decorated a tree. By that Monday, one tree was decorated. Why is that?

69. Straight work shift

Allison worked four hours total on Christmas Eve and eight hours total on Christmas day. She also did a straight 12-hour shift for both days. How did she do it?

70. Timmy's birthday

Timmy's older Brother's birthday was the day before Thanksgiving the previous year and this year. Timmy gets excited about this and figures since his Birthday was the day before Christmas last year, it will be on Christmas day this year. Why was Timmy disappointed on his birthday?

71. Christmas work

Johnny and Adam both leave for work on Christmas morning. Johnny is working just covering a three-hour morning shift at the hospital. Adam has a full day of teaching classes at the high school. Who will be home first?

72. Found in sky and tree top

I am found in the sky, and also the main structure on a tree as I am at the top.

73. Holiday delicacy

I thought I was safe after Thanksgiving, but you proved me wrong. I made my way back to your dinner table on Christmas day, stuffed and with no feathers. What am I?

74. Feet cover

I cover your feet and keep them warm, I may not seem special from the first look, but don't walk on ice without me, or you will slip and fall. What am I?

75. Words that make your day

I may just seem like a piece of paper, but write in me, some beautiful words, and I will make someone's day much better. What am I?

76. Colored sweaters

Tommy is wearing a yellow sweater, one of the three he got for Christmas. The colors of his first two sweaters are dark blue, and medium blue. What is the color of the third sweater?

77. Makes stocking heavy

I make your stocking heavy. I will make your stocking full. If you're not good all year, you will find a lump of me there instead of a gift.

78. Singing carols on neighbors

Mike sang Christmas carols at four different houses, including his own. His house was surrounded by four other houses on each side. He sang to his neighbor on the left, then the neighbor in front of him and then the neighbor to the right of him. Where was the fourth house he went to?

79. The King's painting

I show the final hours of the mighty king. The last time he would eat like a king. Surrounded by his followers, he is aware of what's ahead. I show his last feast, before he lies in his final bed. But alas, I am just a painting in the end, showing the king, with his 12 friends. What am I?

80. Egg drink

I am a sweet and tasty drink. Creamy in my texture, with a touch of eggs. Or maybe a lot of eggs.

81. Savory meal

Your mouth will water as you gaze upon me. Your stomach will be full after you finish me. You will feel like a King when I am served to you. I am a mighty meal, served for many, or just someone who is very hungry. What am I?

82. Mother and son

When you see me, you will see a baby in a manger, born to the mother in the picture. But my real father is not in the picture, he is above in heaven. What am I representing?

83. Numb in the snow

You don't realize that I am there when you're playing in the snow. But don't stay out there too long, as you will get too cold and then I will take a bite out of you, until you can't feel your toes, your fingers and maybe even your nose. What am I?

84. Round snow

I am made of snow, round and cold. You pick me up and pack me tight, and when you get a chance, you throw me at the first target that you can. What am I?

85. Playing with the snow

When you play me, you are the target, they are the target, everyone is the target. You use the snow around you and make a mighty ball. You aim the ball and strike where you can, avoiding those that come your way. If you get hit, you're out of the game. What am I?

86. Throwing snowballs

Tommy makes 10 snowballs. One of them melts and he throws two at a target. He makes five more and throws them all too. Johnny makes five snowballs and gives them to Tommy? Tommy now has 20 snowballs. How many snowballs did Tommy make?

87. Melted snowman

Sam was told by his father not to make a snowman. Sam decided he would sneak out at night and make one, knowing that it would melt by morning because it would be warm the next day. After making the snowman, he dressed it up nicely with a hat and scarf. The next morning, as predicted, the snowman melted, but Sam's father still knew he made the snowman. How did he know?

88. Manger twins but not blood twins

There were two babies born in the manger, but they are not twins. How is this possible?

89. Sweet meat dessert

Despite my name, I have no meat in me. I am sweet to taste. You bake me to perfection. I will be an amazing addition to your Christmas dinner table. But make sure you eat your meal first, as I am a dessert. What am I?

90. Eating mincemeat pies

John is eating two mincemeat pies. One is whole and one is cut up into multiple sections. After eating, the cut-up pie has four slices left, while the other pie is still whole. Which pie has more slices?

91. Melted snowball

How long would a melted snowball take to melt if you put it in the sun?

92. Adorns Christmas trees

I love to adorn your Christmas trees. Without me, you don't even need lights. However, you still can have them. Just hang me good, or I will drop. What am I?

93. Stockings on fireplace

If James hangs four stockings over the fireplace and one falls, how many does he have left?

94. Noel on board

Miley writes the word Noel on the board three times left to right. She points to the word that is on the very left. What is she referring to?

95. Decorates under the Christmas tree

I go under and around the Christmas tree, but I am not a gift. I decorate the tree, but I am not an ornament. I am flashy and colorful, but I am not a light. I am here because that's where they laid my tracks. What am I?

96. In a pear tree

I come from Europe but somehow, they know me round the world. I stay in one spot; you will not see me roaming. But as a bird, you may have heard of me being in a pear tree. What am I?

97. Red pointy on the head

It is cold and snowy on Christmas Day, but because of me, Santa does not need to worry about his head getting cold. I am red and pointy, but no I am not a cone. What am I?

98. Santa does not mail gifts

Why does Santa have to fly to everyone's house individually rather than just mail all the gift?

99. Fire starter

You will find me in a tree, or you will find me in a fireplace. You will use me to start a fire, or you will use me to build a structure. If I am in your fireplace, make sure to put me out before Christmas, otherwise Santa will not be able to get in. What am I?

100. Wishing mate birds

We are birds and we are the same. If you have one of us and find our mate, whatever wish you make will be your fate. What are we?

101. The missing letter

What letter is not in Christmas, even though there is a song about it meaning Christmas.

102. Rolling on snowy hill

An unidentifiable object is rolling down a snowy hill. As it rolls down, it is getting bigger. What is it?

103. The fifth reindeer

Johnny magically turns into a reindeer one day and gets transported to the North Pole. Johnny is with four other reindeer who were magically turned into reindeer. The four reindeers' names are Tammy, Temmy, Timmy and Tommy. What is the fifth reindeers name?

104. Caroling in sweaters

The boy went to his first house for caroling in a blue sweater. The boy went to his first house for caroling in a green sweater. The boy went to his first house for caroling in a green sweater. At this point, the boy in the green sweater had already went caroling at three houses. How did he do it?

105. The Snowman

I am a snowman and I am very cold. In fact, my name even reflects just how cold I am. Who am I?

106. Feel the ground

When reindeer arrive back at the North Pole, how do they feel the ground as they are coming in for a landing?

107. Listen out toy machines

While at the North Pole, how do elves listen out for the toy machines as they are completing the toys?

108. Fast around the world

Who knows how Santa and his reindeer get around the world so fast?

109. Hola, December holiday

I am a phrase, but they say me in Spanish. I mean the same as the festive December holiday in English. What am I called?

110. Dasher and Dancer on drums

Dasher and Dancer were playing on their drum set. They each played with their drum set alone for 30 minutes. They both started at 6:30 PM and finished at 7:00 PM. How did they do it?

111. Holds Christmas tree

I am below the Christmas tree, but I am not a gift. In fact, without me, the Christmas tree would fall. What am I?

112. Reindeer and elf race

Who would win in a foot race between a legless reindeer and a slow elf?

113. Berry beautiful decor

I am green and red, filled with berries. There are boughs of me strewn across the halls, making beautiful decorations. What am I?

114. Elves make toys

If two elves can make 100 toys in an hour, how long will it take four elves to make the same toys?

115. Path without snow

An elf walked through a mile of snow with a shovel. He turned around and walked back on a clear path with no snow How did this happen?

116. Back to North Pole

A reindeer flew 50 miles south from the North Pole. He then turned around and flew 100 miles in the same direction and reached the North Pole. How did he do it?

117. North and South Pole

The North Pole and South Pole have opposite temperatures during the year. On Christmas day, the North Pole has 10 feet of snow. How much snow will the South Pole have?

118. Tall melted snowman

How tall is a melted snowman that was made from 10 feet of snow and was one foot below a nine-foot ceiling?

119. A big leap of faith

If a reindeer is able to leap 100 feet in one try, how far would he have to leap to clear a 25-foot gorge while carrying logs on its back?

120. Log into the fireplace

A reindeer is carrying logs into the house for the fireplace. He is able to carry 50 in about 10 minutes. How fast could he carry the same logs inside using a cart that carries 50 at a time?

121. Elves bake cookies

Two elves bake a dozen cookies each and eat them. How many cookies will they have to give to Santa if they give him half of their cookies?

122. Christmas babies

Chuck's mom has five children who were all born on
Christmas Day. She names her first four kids Noel, Nael,
Neel and Neil. What is the fifth child's name?

123. Born not twins

Two girls have the same mother. They were born on
Christmas day, at the same time and in the same hospital.
But they are not twins. How is this possible?

Chapter 2: Hard Riddles

"One of the Most Glorious Messes in The World is the Mess Created in the Living Room on Christmas Day. Don't Clean It Up Too Quickly." ~ Andy Rooney

124. Claus during Christmas

I live in the North Pole. My last name is Claus. I bring Christmas cheer to everyone. I won't be at your house on Christmas though. Who am I?

125. Mrs. Claus makes cookies

Mrs. Claus makes 12 cookies for Santa. Santa shared one with each of the nine reindeer, and then he ate the rest of the 11. How did he do it?

126. Walk the tree lot

There are 12 trees in a lot and 12 people walked up to them. Each took a tree. Now there are 11 trees left. How is this possible?

127. Christmas on board

Tommy wrote out the word Christmas on the board in white chalk. What phrase was he representing?

128. Peace on Earth

Tommy was on a role, so he drew the planet Earth on the board and then the peace symbol on top of it. What does this represent?

129. Decorated tree

On Christmas day, the tree was completely decorated but nobody knew who did it. James went to church; Sally went to the library and Phyllis went to her friend's house. Everyone was somewhere when the tree got decorated. Who probably did it?

130. Edible man

I am a man that you can eat. What am I?

131. Parade with friends

James went to the Christmas parade with four of his friends. They bought five tickets total for Nappy, Neppy, Nippy and Noppy. Who was the fifth ticket for?

132. Gift oil to Jesus

I am an essential oil, also believed to be given as a gift to Jesus. What am I?

133. Nocturnal glimmer

I work all night and I sleep all day. I dazzle the neighborhood with my glimmer. People get in their car and drive around just to look at me and all of my coworkers. What am I?

134. Devoured by Santa

Santa eats so many of me by the start of Christmas morning that he is sick and tired and can't even look at me until the next year. What am I?

135. Santa's post

What is Santa's favorite post?

136. Walk away from North Pole

Santa walked 10 miles south away from the North Pole. He is now 1000 miles away from the North Pole. How did he do it?

137. Santa went camping

When Santa and his elves go camping, what do they have cooking over the campfire?

138. Santa in Antarctica

When you go to the continent of Antarctica, how are you able to find the exact measurements and geographical location of Santa's home?

139. My friend Carol

If your friend Carol is all decked out in her holiday clothing mixed with a Santa hat, Christmas sweated and bells, what do you call her?

140. Ornament giveaways

Darrin pulls out 10 ornaments from an empty box. How many would he give Jan if he were to give her half of them?

141. Put on hands over cat name

You put me on over your hands on a cold Christmas night, and you can also name your cat after me. What am I?

142. Pairs of mittens

Jake has three pairs of mittens and he gives one mitten to Janice to wear. How many mittens does he have left?

143. Helps Santa walk

If Santa Claus twists his ankle, what will he use to help him walk?

144. Three Mathematicians

What do you call three men who are able to solve a math problem easily?

145. Reindeer on other holiday

Which one of Santa's reindeer also works another holiday?

146. House from canes

Santa builds a new house using 20 life size candy canes. The house is 2000 square feet. How many of those candy canes can he use to build a 1000 square foot house?

147. Santa left North Pole

When Santa leaves the North Pole, he flies 100 miles South, takes a turn and flies one hundred miles east, then flies 100 miles north and then another 100 miles west. Where did Santa end up?

148. Snowman went missing

A man is talking to his new friend, who is a Snowman. The snowman looks depressed. The man asks him what is wrong. The Snowman replies that all he knows is cold weather. For once, he would love to spend Christmas in a warm climate. The man decided it's time to take the snowman to Hawaii or some fun in the sun. When they arrive, the man could not find his new Snowman friend. What happened?

149. Gingerbread house

Tommy and Bill built a life size gingerbread house in one day. How long will it take to build the house is Mike and Chuck join them?

150. Shorter as it gets older

I am small and slender. I can light up a room when I am on. I start off tall when I am young, but I grow shorter as I get older. What Am I?

151. Jingles all the way

I am a musical instrument and you can hear me jingling from miles away as Santa comes into to town and gives gifts away. What am I?

152. Look like Santa

The elementary school teacher with pure white hair wanted to surprise his students on Christmas Day by growing a large beard to look like Santa. What will be the kids' reactions when he shows up?

153. Suspenders and belt

Why does Santa wear suspenders and a black belt?

154. Sleigh weight limit

What is the weight limit of Santa's sleigh?

155. Baking sugar cookies

The mom baked 20 sugar cookies in 15 minutes at 350 degrees. How long will it take to bake the same cookies at 400 degrees?

156. Comet and Cupid

Comet and Cupid walk outside and walk 20 steps from the door. They are now 40 steps away from each other. How did this happen?

157. Christmas or New Year

Jamie is wondering what she will celebrate first during the year, Christmas or New Year. What is his answer?

158. Light rays across sky

Santa, Mrs. Claus and all of their reindeers are standing around watching the stars. They see a flashing light rays across the sky. Mrs. Claus says, "Wow, that looked like a Comet? What does Santa say?

159. Reindeers play football

All of the reindeers were playing a game of touch football. All except for one, because of the way he looks, they excluded him from any reindeer games. Who was it?

160. Breakfast with the elves

Mrs. Claus cooks breakfast for all of the elves and her husband. She cooks eleven different meals for eleven elves. Santa and the elves begin eating. Did everyone get a breakfast?

161. Candy canes in a box

Jenny has five candy canes in a box. She gives out five candy canes evenly to five of her friends and one is still left in the box. How is this possible?

162. Baked fruits

I am filled with fruits, but I am not a tree. You bake me. In fact, a lot of people don't like me. What am I?

163. Reindeer with another job

Christmas was tight this year. I was barely able to make enough to pay my rent up at the North Pole. I work as a reindeer, but I have to get a second job. The title of which is in my name. What is it?

164. Fruitcake for eveyone

Jim cut the fruitcake in five even pieces. Everyone took a piece, and now there are four left. How is this possible?

165. Favorite veggie

What is a snowman's favorite vegetable?

166. Snowman sees

How does a snowman see?

167. Built a snowman

Timmy built a snowman that is eight feet tall. How much snow would he need to build the same snowman again?

168. Play on Christmas

Billy wants to see a play on Christmas, but both of his parents work full time. One is a doctor and one is a teacher. Who will be able to take him to the play?

169. Best friend Nick

You have a best friend named Nick, who is always kind and giving to other people. What do people call your friend Nick, that portrays his giving behavior?

170. East to West

You are sliding down a mountain going East. Suddenly, you are headed West. How did this happen?

171. Bill's mistletoes

Bill has three mistletoes. He puts two on the top of different doors. He puts the third in the basement. How many mistletoes does he have left?

172. Baker's dozen of gingerbread

Suzy makes a baker's dozen of gingerbread men. She gives seven away and now she has how many left?

173. Fairest of them all.

How do you keep an unbreakable ornament from shattering when it falls off the tree?

174. Christmas car

Grandma gives Jimmy a car for Christmas. He keeps it on the mantle. How does it fit there?

175. Christmas tree decors

The Christmas Tree is adorned with these, but they do not light up.

176. Simultaneous dinner

Bobby goes to Jimmy and his cousin's house at the exact same time for Christmas dinner. How did he do it?

177. Ancient GPS

There was no GPS then, but I was there to help guide the three Wise Men to Jerusalem. When they saw me, they knew what direction to go. What am I?

178. Fibbing Billy

Billy met Santa at the mall. Santa asked Billy how the year went. Billy told him all of the great stuff that he did. However, Santa knew that Billy was fibbing. How did he know?

179. Holiday errands

Jill has two days on December 25th and the 26th to take care of some errands. She has to go to the post office to mail an important package and to the mall to buy some new clothes. How should she plan it out?

180. Cracks hard shells

I am mostly used as a decoration. But as I stand tall, with my large hat and stoic demeanor, know that I am also able to crack some hard shells.

181. Busiest workplace on Christmas

I am the busiest working area during Christmas time. Where more toys are made than all of the factories in the world combined. What am I?

182. Bald Santa

A child is awoken in the middle of the night and sees Santa. She yells, "Santa, you're bald!" What did Santa forget?

183. Gift boxes

Tommy opened one of his Christmas gift boxes. After opening the first box, both of his hands had gifts in them. How did this happen?

184. Snowman's multiple jobs

The snowman worked at the North Pole, but he needed a second job to make ends meet. His choices are the closed down snow making factory, or a lifeguard at the beach. Which one should he choose?

185. Fibbing Dasher

Dasher tells Santa that Rudolph is hiding in the small room with the lights turned off. When Santa walks by it, he sees darkness, but knows that Dasher is fibbing. How does he know?

186. Rudolph's right way

How does Rudolph always go the right way on Christmas Eve?

187. Faster than the human eye

If Santa travels faster than the human eye can see, how can we see him when looking out of our bedroom window?

188. Elves' hearing range

Elves have very strong hearing due to their pointy ears. How far in the distance can the elf with the missing ears hear?

189. Most understanding woman

Who is the most understanding woman on Christmas?

190. Christmas Knight

The teacher draws a Knight in his attire on the chalkboard, and after it, she writes the word Christmas. What is she trying to say?

191. Gone on the day

I appear at the beginning of Christmas, only once in December but never on the day of Christmas. What am I?

192. Three Christmases

Christmas occurred for Billy three times while he was in his house. How did this happen?

193. Few minutes but next day

Santa left the North Pole at 11:55 and came back 10 minutes later the next day. How did he do it?

194. Vigilant Santa

How come no one has ever caught Santa while he is putting gifts under the tree?

195. Workaholic Santa

If Santa only works on Christmas and works 20 hours in a day, when will he rest?

196. Candy cane boxes

Mikey bought 2 boxes of candy canes. He left one box in his car and left one at his house. How many boxes does he have left?

197. Santa lands on boots

When Santa lands on someone's roof with his special boots, how is he able to feel the ground below him when he gets out of his sleigh?

198. Code his whereabouts

Mary is trying to tell her friend where Santa is using only a code. She draws a house, then she draws an arrow pointing up on top of the roof. What does this mean?

199. Christmas prior New Year

We know that Christmas come before Thanksgiving in the dictionary, but where does Christmas come before New Year?

200. Generous gifts for holiday

I am a very generous person. In fact, I give my love many gifts for 12 days during the Christmas Holiday. What song is about me?

201. Eggs for everyone

Billy allowed his friends to use his eggs in the fridge for what they needed. John used two to make eggnog. Ida used three for her cake. Tim used one for his milkshake. When Billy looked, there were only five eggs missing, when there should have been six. Who did not use an egg?

Chapter 3: Difficult Riddles

"Never worry about the size of your Christmas tree. In the eyes of children, they are all 30 feet tall." ~ Larry Wilde, The Merry Book of Christmas

202. Keep the doctor away

When Santa first met Mrs. Claus, he was worried about losing her to a doctor because he would be away for seven days and would not see her. But he had a plan. Before leaving, he gave Mrs. Claus seven apples, and when he came back, she was still there for him. Why is that?

203. Four gifts under the tree

Jimmy opened his first present on Christmas morning. He has four gifts total. The three under the tree are wrapped in blue wrapping paper. What color is the fourth one wrapped in?

204. Supernatural made of snow

How do you make a supernatural being in the snow?

205. Like Santa but no beard

Who wears a red coat, black boots, a red hat, and has no beard?

206. Santa tracker

How does Santa keep track of every house in the world that he has to deliver gifts to?

207. Working sleigh on holiday

If Santa's sleigh does not work 364 days a year, how will he be able to get around on Christmas?

208. Winged watcher

I look like you, but I am other worldly. You may not see me, but I am watching over you with my wide wingspan. What am I?

209. Last seat on plane

An angel and an elf are trying to get the last seat on an airplane. Who will they give it to in order for both of them to get to their destination?

210. Christmas work shift

James is working on Christmas eve for 8 hours and Christmas Day for 4 hours. He is working a 12-hour shift starting on Christmas Eve. How is this possible?

211. Sleigh weight loss

When Santa and his reindeer set out on Christmas Eve night, The sleigh weighs 1,000,000 pounds. When they return to the North Pole, it weighs 1,000 pounds. What happened to all of the weight?

212. Elves pull the sleigh

How many elves does it take to pull the sleigh?

213. Cool down the drinks

The elves want to cool down their drinks, and their choices are to put them outside, where it's 30 degrees, or inside the broken fridge, which can go down to 10 degrees. What is the better option?

214. No elves in South pole

How come you never see elves at the South Pole?

215. Common in both poles

What will you find in the North Pole and the South Pole, never in the desert, usually high in the mountains and always in the freezer?

216. Santa's pet

What does Santa have as a pet?

217. Poor treatment of snowman

What do you call a snowman who treats others poorly?

218. Santa's pop quiz

If Santa gave a pop quiz with only one question, what would that question   be? It's the only thing he really needs to know about you.

219. Red velvet cupcakes

Rudolph ate all of Santa's red velvet cupcakes. The remnants of the cupcakes were all over Rudolph's nose. But Santa did not know he ate them. How is this possible?

220. Sharp-hearing elves

Why are Elves hearing so sharp?

221. 5th day jewelry gift

What type of jewelry would Santa give to Mrs. Clause five days after Christmas?

222. Santa's favorite instrument

What is Santa's favorite musical instrument?

223. Egg hoarding for Christmas

Why do Elves buy so many eggs during Christmas time?

224. Dandruff on snowman

What do you call dandruff on a snowman?

225. Snowman winter games

If a snowman were to play some winter games, what would their best event be? The sport they were born to play.

226. Drink cover on a snowman

I am found on the face of a snowman. I also cover your drinks when you are not drinking them. What am I?

227. Two missing reindeers

All of the reindeer are playing cards. You have the one with the red nose, the one that dashes quickly, the one that dances gracefully, the one that walks with the spring in their step, the one that's a little mischievous, The one that moves like a star in the sky and the one that unites lovers. Which two reindeer are missing?

228. Deep fog on Christmas

Santa and his reindeer set out on the cold dark night. The fog is so deep they cannot see. Will they be able to go out on Christmas?

229. Church with basement

There is a two-story church building with a basement. The first story is decorated with lights and candles. The second story is decorated with streamers. Is there a third story for you to decorate?

230. With dance recital

Santa is playing a game of softball with all of his reindeer. One of them cannot make it because he has a dance recital. Which one is it?

231. All the way to cosmos

One of Santa's reindeer's name suggests he can hit a ball all the way into the cosmos. Which reindeer is it?

232. Skips in step to base

One of Santa's reindeer has a skip in his step as he ran to the bases. Which one is it?

233. Moves fastest to base

The reindeer that can move through the bases the fastest. Which one is it?

234. Went to work out

Santa went to the gym on Christmas. He worked out for two hours and came home the day after Christmas. How did he do it?

235. Elf went to gym

A three-foot elf went to the gym, and he tried doing pullups on the six-foot bar. Santa had to assist him first. In what way did he have to help him?

236. Ring like Christmas tree

I am just like your Christmas tree; except I am a ring, like what you wear on your fingers. What am I?

237. Mr. Scrooge's visitor

I am the first to visit the old man, Mr. Scrooge. I show him how things used to be, in hopes that he will change his ways. I visit Mr. Scrooge second, and I show him how other people see him at the moment. I visit Mr. Scrooge last, and I show him what will be if he continues his present path. Who are we?

238. Santa's clue

If you do not make this, Santa will not know what you want. What is it?

239. Household rodent

I am your everyday household rodent, and I move from hole to hole. I am in everyone's house all year long. However, on the night before Christmas, not even I can be seen, because not a creature was stirring, not even me. What am I?

240. Singing from mountain top

My heart was small, but after I saw them singing, even when they lost it all, my heart grew big, and I was a changed man. I live on a mountain top, away from all of them, but now that I see the true meaning of Christmas, I will join them. Who am I?

241. Elf soup

What is an elf's favorite soup?

242. In the freezer

I am all over the North Pole. You can also find me in your freezer, but not your fridge. What am I?

243. Season of snow

You can find me in magical fairy tales. I am a season that brings beautiful snow and chilly weather. But if you don't wear a jacket, you will not like me one bit. What am I?

244. Common degrees

Zero degrees, negative 10 degrees and 2 degrees are different numbers. But how are they the same?

245. Earth destination

I am a destination on Earth. You can find me at the top of Canada, or even Alaska. Heck, I am even in Russia. But you will not find me Egypt. Where am I?

246. Spiky roof decor

I decorate your roof ever so fancy, but don't let me fall on you; I am ever so spiky. What am I?

247. Keeps the doctor away

I am in your favorite pie. I can live on a tree or in your pantry. I come in a variety of colors. One of me a day, will keep the doctor away. What am I?

248. Snow slider

People will fall through the snow when they are standing on it, but when they sit on me, they will slide down with speed. What am I?

249. Non-living pointy ears

I am small and green. I have pointy ears, and I look at you clean. But I am not alive. What am I?

250. Ran up the hill

The reindeer ran up a long hill. He then turned around and ran up again. How did he do it?

251. Easter egg color

If the wreath is green, the Christmas tree is green, the lights are green, and the garland is green, what is the color of the Easter Eggs?

252. Not Mr. Scrooge

I am the opposite emotion of Mr. Scrooge.

253. Color me crazy

You can fill me in whatever way you want, but since I have Santa and the elves on me, Christmas colors will look best. What am I?

254. Shovel the driveway

Billy's mom asks him to shovel the driveway after the snow is melted. If it takes 10 minutes to shovel half of the driveway, how long will it take to shovel the whole driveway?

255. Old and greedy man

I am old, I am greedy, I do not care for Christmas and those who may need me. I live in my own world and want nothing to do with others. Until one day, I get some visitors, and I change my whole outlook. Who am I?

256. Home decoration

A snowman is decorating his home. What does he not want to stand close to?

257. From fallen cold crystals

I was once tall and proud. I was made from the cold crystals that fall from the sky. Now, I am a slip and slide. What am I?

258. Big white bearded man

I am sitting at a desk, stroking my big white beard. I am looking through my list and making decisions. Will he get this, and will she get that. I am looking through and deciding now. Who am I, and what am I doing?

259. Candy trading

I am filled with treats. I will fill you up. I am a kid's second favorite place on Christmas, after the toy store. What am I?

260. Christmas before Thanksgiving

Christmas always follows Thanksgiving in a calendar year, but where does it come before Thanksgiving?

261. Santa is coming to town

Santa comes into the town Friday, stays three days and leaves Friday. How did he do it?

262. Parent holiday

I am another name associated with a jolly red guy, and it relates to being a parent. What is it?

263. Letting go the past

I am what occurs when you forget what others have done to you. Letting go and moving on is what I am about and not letting the pains of the past harm you any longer. What am I?

264. Neck ornament

I am a decorative item. I can be worn around a person's head or neck, or I can be laid on top of an inanimate object, like a Christmas tree. What am I?

265. Neck thermal

Wear me around your neck when it is freezing cold. Wrap me tight, but not too tight and have my design show the Christmas holiday in full form. What am I?

266. Artificial trees

Micah has two trees: an artificial one and a real one. They are both the same size. Which one will take longer to assemble?

267. Candy canes on tree

Mike hangs 20 candy canes on the Christmas tree. The next morning. He grabs two candy canes and eats them. Mike still has 20 candy canes left on the tree. How is this possible?

268. Holiday pessimist

I am a popular Christmas figure representing a lot of the negativities of the holidays. I have a scowl and poor outlook on life. However, after getting some unexpected visitors, my mindset completely changes. Who am I?

269. First fall from the sky

My first fall of the year from the sky represents the beautiful holiday some your way and a change in seasons. What am I?

270. Annual tradition

Jimmy and his dad have a yearly tradition of decorating the Christmas tree the night before Christmas. This year, they also built a gingerbread house for the first time. They realize that they don't have time to do both. What will they do the next year?

271. Travel buddy

They're flying in, they're flying out. It's nonstop motion, there's no doubt. If you want to travel far and wide, you will likely have to pass through me at some point. It's Christmas time, so don't expect to be anywhere on time. What am I?

272. Less loved

Don't forget about me this holiday season. I may have less than you but am still filled with love. I just need an extra hand, to help me rise above. Who am I?

273. Share canes to friends

Jenny has three candy canes to share. She gives one to both of her friends. Now she has two. How is this possible?

274. Round yellow jewelry

I am round, I am yellow, I may be jewelry or something around a beautiful bird's neck. On Christmas day, I am given as a gift with four other things that look like me. What am I?

275. Field reindeers

Tommy is walking alone in a field next to a reindeer. When Santa looks in the same field, he sees two reindeer. How is this possible?

276. Homeless Adam

An unknown man was found at the North Pole. Santa and his elves helped him up. He was not wearing a shirt, so he must have been freezing. As soon as they saw him, though, they knew he was Adam. How did they know?

277. Empty cookie box

One of Santa's elves knew that Santa kept some cookies in his desk. One day, he snuck in to take one. One turned into two, which turned into five. All the cookies were gone. The elf panicked and quickly threw the empty box in the trash. Santa was curious about what happened. While he was walking around, he looked at the side of the elf's workstation and found out the answer. How did he know?

278. Fake reindeers

The people of the Earth saw Santa walking a long distance with his reindeer to get across very vast lands. How did they know they were not really reindeers?

279. Trees play baseball

If two Christmas trees are playing baseball, what will they use as the ball?

280. Tree salon

Where does a Christmas tree go for a haircut?

281. Carrot and bottle cap debris

A man is walking in his back yard after a snowstorm. Suddenly, he steps on a carrot and a bottle cap. Why were those there?

282. Throws snowballs on halls

A snowman is throwing solid snowballs at the halls in his home. Why is he doing this?

283. Race to finish line

Who would win in a race between Santa Clause and the fastest person in the world?

284. Three important persons

Who are the three most important people in Santa's life?

285. Snowman illness

What is the most common illness to hit a snowman?

286. Ball but doesn't bounce

You can throw me like a ball, catch me like a ball, or carry me like a ball. But you can't bounce me, hit me, or kick me. I will just explode. What am I?

287. Inflatable replica

I am red, I am jolly, I am smiling, and I am giving cheer. The only thing is, I am full of hot air. I am not the real thing, but a perfect replica you can put in your front yard. What am I?

288. Something to wear

I am a Christmas gift under the tree. As soon as you pick me up and feel the soft packaging, you know exactly what I am. You may not like me, but you need me, because otherwise, you will have nothing to wear. What am I?

289. Dasher's favorite song

What is Dasher's favorite song?

290. Not so smart phone

Santa was carrying his smart cell phone for directions, trying not to be noticed. As he flew through the night, quickly and quietly, he came back to the North Pole seemingly unnoticed. However, when he looked outside, he saw a crown of people who knew where he was. How did they find him?

291. When right went wrong

Santa was on his sleigh, and he was turning right. He continued to travel right. He made more right turns. He turned right again then turned the other way and then made a right turn again. Suddenly, Santa was lost. Where did he go wrong?

292. Elves hiding spot

When traveling to the South Pole, what is the easiest way to find the Elves hiding spot?

293. Reindeers won't slip on ice

When traveling across the globe, how do the reindeer not slip on the ice from all of the snow?

294. Reindeers play football

Santa and his reindeer are playing a game of touch football. Rudolph never plays with the other eight reindeer, because of his shiny nose. On this day, there are nine players total when there are usually eight. Who is the ninth player if Rudolph never plays?

295. Insufficient thermal effect

Santa is wearing warm boots a coat and a hat. He is all bundled up. He gets frostbite though. What happened?

296. Elf tracker

How does Santa keep track of all of his elves?

297. Blitzen the reindeer

How would Blitzen guide the sleigh if his red nose no longer shines?

298. The likely gesture

How do you know if a reindeer likes you?

299. All women's dinner

Two mothers, two daughters and one grandmother go out for Christmas dinner. There are a total of three people in the group. How is this possible?

300. Cane eating time

Jimmy's parents gave him five candy canes and told him not to eat them until Christmas Day. After opening his gifts on Christmas morning, how much longer will Jimmy have to wait before eating the candy canes?

301. He is my son

Billy's dad is working in his office on Christmas day. Billy has no babysitter, so he goes to work with his dad, but cannot go into his office. He takes a walk down the hall and goes into another office. A person at the door stops Billy and says he cannot come in. Someone from behind says, "It is ok, he is my son." How is this possible if Billy's dad was in a completely different office?

Chapter 4: Easy Riddle Answers

1.
Answer: Snowman.

2.
Answer: Tree.

3.
Answer: Christmas Time.

4.
Answer: Christmas Time.

5.
Answer: None. The tree is already decorated.

6.
Answer: Headphones.

7.
Answer: Christmas Carol.

8.
Answer: Snow.

9.
Answer: Marshmallow.

10.
Answer: Candy Cane.

11.
Answer: None. He already bought it with marshmallows in it.

12.
Answer: Elf.

Christmas Riddles

13.
Answer: Peppermint.

14.
Answer: Kully. Covers the five vowels.

15.
Answer: Billy. He would not be raking leaves on a cold Christmas night.

16.
Answer: Rudolph the Red-Nosed Reindeer, and I have a very shiny nose.

17.
Answer: Mistletoe.

18.
Answer: Apple Cider.

19.
Answer: Chimney; and make sure to put the fire out on Christmas Eve night.

20.
Answer: Wrapping Paper.

21.
Answer: Gingerbread House.

22.
Answer: Donner does not have a shiny red nose.

23.
Answer: Black ice.

24.
Answer: Your Christmas Gift.

25.
Answer: Santa's Sleigh.

26.
Answer: He ate the bottom half of two cookies and the top half of the other two, allowing him to join the different halves into a single cookie.

27.
Answer: When the sleigh is parked, it is not moving at all.

28.
Answer: Santa's workshop.

29.
Answer: Stocking.

30.
Answer: Santa's Reindeer.

31.
Answer: Christmas Card.

32.
Answer: In his house. He walked uphill from his driveway. So, all he had to do was walk back down to get to his house.

33.
Answer: The same trees are already chopped down. He won't need to use a chainsaw to chop them down again.

34.
Answer: Fireplace.

35.
Answer: Ice skates.

36.
Answer: Stocking stuffer.

37.
Answer: Caroler.

38.
Answer: Four members of a family go caroling, but they don't go to the same houses together.

39.
Answer: Snowbank.

40.
Answer: Dinner.

41.
Answer: He would not have decorated the stairs. It is a one-story house.

42.
Answer: Neither one. It is an artificial tree. He can buy it from a store.

43.
Answer: He won't have to take it down the stairs since the tree is on the first floor.

44.
Answer: He does not have to do anything if the dog is just running around his front yard. His Snowman is in the backyard.

45.

Answer: Johnny has nothing to worry about. He ate all of his candy canes. There is nothing left for his little brother to take.

46.
Answer: His fourth wish is to set the Ferry free like she asked. He just got one extra wish beyond the three.

47.
Answer: He does not have to wake up his kids. He wants to leave before they are awake.

48.
Answer: She still has two Christmas trees. One of them just fell, but she still has it.

49.
Answer: Nothing. Clocks do not talk.

50.
Answer: They still have a total of 10 candy canes left. They just swapped them between each other but did not get rid of any.

51.
Answer: He just grabbed them from the bag that was on the ground. The star was not on top of the tree yet.

52.
Answer: The dictionary.

53.
Answer: Because he is Santa Claus, he knows when you are sleeping, and he knows when you are awake.

54.
Answer: First place, since he does win the race.

55.
Answer: It is a different James' house.

56.
Answer: Easy; you just ask for it. Just like any other day. Let's not complicate things.

57.
Answer: Jane.

58.
Answer: His special coat was gone.

59.
Answer: None. The cookies will be for Santa.

60.
Answer: Tinsel.

61.
Answer: One of his cousins lives with him.

62.
Answer: New Year.

63.
Answer: It is an 8-ounce glass, but he only fills it partly.

64.
Answer: Plum pudding.

65.
Answer: Punch.

66.

Answer: The cup that is not full is Jamie's. She had been drinking her punch, but her friend set it down on the table immediately after pouring.

67.
Answer: Ribbon.

68.
Answer: All is the name of the person who decorated just one tree.

69.
Answer: She started her shift on Christmas Eve night at 8 PM, worked four hours until midnight, and then worked an additional eight hours.

70.
Answer: Christmas is always on a set date, unlike Thanksgiving. So, Timmy's birthday will always be the day before Christmas.

71.
Answer: Adam. The high school won't be open on Christmas Day.

72.
Answer: Star.

73.
Answer: Turkey.

74.
Answer: Snow boots.

75.
Answer: Christmas card.

76.

Answer: Yellow. The one he is wearing.

77.
Answer: Coal.

78.
Answer: The fourth house he sang at was his own.

79.
Answer: The Last Supper painting.

80.
Answer: Eggnog.

81.
Answer: A Feast.

82.
Answer: Nativity Scene.

83.
Answer: Frostbite.

84.
Answer: Snowball.

85.
Answer: Snowball fight.

86.
Answer: Tommy originally made 10, then another five and then received some from friends and threw some at targets. He then received five more from Johnny. After all this, he would have had 13 snowballs. Since he has 20, that would be an additional seven that he made. Making the total 22 snowballs that he made personally.

87.
Answer: The hat and scarf were still there, even though the snowman melted.

88.
Answer: They were both born in the same manger, but not on the same day.

89.
Answer: Mincemeat Pie.

90.
Answer: The cut-up pie as it has four slices and the whole pie has no slices as it is still whole.

91.
Answer: No time. It is melted already.

92.
Answer: Ornament.

93.
Answer: He still has four.

94.
Answer: The first Noel.

95.
Answer: Toy train.

96.
Answer: Partridge.

97.
Answer: Santa's hat.

98.

Christmas Riddles

Answer: Because the Post Office is closed on Christmas.

99.
Answer: Fire log.

100.
Answer: Two turtle doves.

101.
Answer: There's no L.

102.
Answer: A snowball.

103.
Answer: Johnny is the fifth reindeer.

104.
Answer: It was his first time caroling in a green sweater. But he also went to one house in a blue sweater and a red sweater.

105.
Answer: Frosty the Snowman.

106.
Answer: With their feet.

107.
Answer: With their ears.

108.
Answer: Only Santa and his reindeer and that is how it will stay.

109.
Answer: Feliz Navidad.

110.

Answer: They both played at the same time, but on their own drum set.

111.
Answer: Christmas tree stand.

112.
Answer: The elf since the reindeer is legless.

113.
Answer: Holly.

114.
Answer: No time since the toys are already made.

115.
Answer: He was shoveling the snow as he was walking.

116.
Answer: He was already 50 miles away from the North Pole when he started going South.

117.
Answer: None. Since it is opposite.

118.
Answer: Zero feet, since the snowman is melted.

119.
Answer: Easy, just 25 feet to clear the gorge.

120.
Answer: No time. He won't have to carry the same logs inside.

121.
Answer: None, since they ate the cookies after baking them.

122.
Answer: Chuck.

123.
Answer: They were not born on the same year. Everything else is the same.

Chapter 5: Hard Riddle Answers

124.
Answer: Mrs. Claus.

125.
Answer: He shared just one of his 12 cookies with all of his reindeer.

126.
Answer: Each is the name of the person who took just one tree.

127.
Answer: White Christmas.

128.
Answer: World Peace.

129.
Answer: Sally. The library would have been closed on Christmas.

130.
Answer: Gingerbread Man.

131.
Answer: James.

132.
Answer: Frankincense.

133.
Answer: Christmas Lights.

134.
Answer: Cookies.
135.

Christmas Riddles

Answer: The North Pole.

136.
Answer: He was already 990 miles South from the North Pole.
He just walked another 10 miles.

137.
Answer: Chestnuts roasting on an open fire.

138.
Answer: You can't. First you have to get in the right area. Santa
lives on the North Pole.

139.
Answer: Christmas Carol.

140.
Answer: None. He pulls ornaments out of an empty box, so he
has none.

141.
Answer: Mittens

142.
Answer: Five. He has three pairs, which equals six. He only gives
one mitten to Janice, so he now has five.

143.
Answer: His Candy Cane

144.
Answer: Three Wisemen

145.
Answer: Cupid on Valentine's Day

146.

Answer: None. He already used them to build a house and can't use them again.

147.
Answer: Right back at the North Pole. He just went the same distance in all directions and made a square to get back to the North Pole.

148.
Answer: The snowman disappeared. They can only live where it snows.

149.
Answer: None. The house is already built.

150.
Answer: Candle.

151.
Answer: Sleigh bell.

152.
Answer: No reaction. The kids won't be at school.

153.
Answer: To keep his clothes on.

154.
Answer: No weight Limit. It is magical.

155.
Answer: No time. The cookies are already baked.

156.
Answer: They each walked 20 steps, just in the opposite direction.

Christmas Riddles

157.
Answer: New Year, because New Year technically falls before Christmas on the calendar year.

158.
Answer: No, Comet is standing next to me.

159.
Answer: Rudolph. They still won't let him play in any reindeer games.

160.
Answer: No. Santa took one. That just leaves 10 meals between 11 elves. Someone did not get breakfast.

161.
Answer: She gave the last candy cane to her friend while still in the box.

162.
Answer: Fruitcake.

163.
Answer: Dancer.

164.
Answer: Everyone is that name of the person who took the piece of cake.

165.
Answer: Carrots. They usually eat it as their melting.

166.
Answer: He can't, because he does not have real eyes.

167.

Answer: None. He won't have to build the same snowman again.

168.
Answer: The teacher. They won't have to work on Christmas Day.

169.
Answer: Saint Nick.

170.
Answer: The hill has a curve in it.

171.
Answer: He still has three.

172.
Answer: Six. Because a Baker's dozen is 13.

173.
Answer: Nothing. It is unbreakable.

174.
Answer: It is a toy car.

175.
Answer: Ornaments.

176.
Answer: Jimmy and his cousin live in the same house.

177.
Answer: Christmas star.

178.
Answer: Because he is Santa and he knows if you've been bad or good.

Christmas Riddles

179.
Answer: Go to the mall on the 25th and the post office on the 26th. The post office will be closed on the 25th.

180.
Answer: Nutcracker.

181.
Answer: Santa's workshop.

182.
Answer: His hat.

183.
Answer: There was more than one gift in the box.

184.
Answer: Well, he would have to work as a lifeguard. The snow making factory is closed down. This should get interesting.

185.
Answer: He cannot see Rudolph's bright red nose.

186.
Answer: By never going the wrong way.

187.
Answer: Since he moves too fast, we will never be able to see him.

188.
Answer: He can't because his ears are missing.

189.
Answer: Mrs. Claus.

190.
Answer: The Knight Before Christmas.

191.
Answer: The letter C. No matter what day of the week Christmas is, the letter C is never in that day.

192.
Answer: Billy lived in his house during three different Christmases on three different years.

193.
Answer: He left at 11:55 at night and came back at 12:05 AM the next day.

194.
Answer: Because he only comes in when he knows people are sleeping and will leave when he knows they are awake.

195.
Answer: The rest of the year.

196.
Answer: He still has two boxes.

197.
Answer: With his feet.

198.
Answer: Santa is up on the roof top.

199.
Answer: Also in the Dictionary. During the year, Christmas actually comes after New Year since New Year is January 1st and Christmas is December 25th.

200.

Christmas Riddles

Answer: The 12 days of Christmas.

201.
Answer: Tim. He would not need it for a milkshake.

Chapter 6: Difficult Riddle Answers

202.
Answer: An apple a day keeps the doctor away.

203.
Answer: It's not wrapped in anything. Jimmy has already opened that gift.

204.
Answer: Lay on the ground and make snow angels.

205.
Answer: Santa, after he has shaved.

206.
Answer: He writes it in his Yule Log.

207.
Answer: Since there are 365 days in a year and the sleight does not work 364 of them, Santa will still be able to use the sleigh on Christmas Day.

208.
Answer: An Angel.

209.
Answer: The elf. The angel can fly on their own.

210.
Answer: He will work eight hours on Christmas Eve, starting at 4 PM and working until midnight. He will then work an additional four hours starting midnight on Christmas Day.

Christmas Riddles

211.
Answer: Easy, he dropped off all of his gifts, so now the sleigh weighs much less than before.

212.
Answer: None. The elves don't pull the sleigh, the reindeers do.

213.
Answer: Outside, since the fridge is broken.

214.
Answer: Because they live in the North Pole.

215.
Answer: Ice.

216.
Answer: Polar Bear. Really, the only pet he can have.

217.
Answer: Abominable Snowman

218.
Answer: Have you been Naughty or nice?

219.
Answer: Rudolph's red nose was the same color as the red cake.

220.
Answer: They have pointy ears.

221.
Answer: Five golden Rings.

222.
Answer: Jingle Bells.

223.
Answer: They love their Eggnog.

224.
Answer: Snowflakes.

225.
Answer: Snow shoeing.

226.
Answer: Bottle caps.

227.
Answer: Donner and Blitzen. It's hard to describe their names in just words.

228.
Answer: Yes, Rudolph is with them and has a shiny red nose.

229.
Answer: Yes, you will. There is a third story. It is the basement.

230.
Answer: Dancer, just like his name says.

231.
Answer: Comet.

232.
Answer: Prancer.

233.
Answer: Dasher. He just dashes through them.

234.
Answer: He went to the gym late at night shortly before midnight, then came back home after midnight the next day.

235.
Answer: He had to boost him up. He could not reach the six-foot bar.

236.
Answer: A wreath.

237.
Answer: The Ghost of Christmas Past, present and future.

238.
Answer: Christmas Wish List.

239.
Answer: A mouse.

240.
Answer: The Grinch who stole Christmas.

241.
Answer: Elf-abet Soup.

242.
Answer: Ice.

243.
Answer: Season of Winter.

244.
Answer: They are all extremely cold.

245.
Answer: The Arctic Circle.

246.
Answer: Icicle.

247.
Answer: An Apple.

248.
Answer: Sled.

249.
Answer: Elf on a shelf.

250.
Answer: After running up a hill, he turned around, but not all of the way. The direction he turned, he could still run going up.

251.
Answer: There won't be any Easter eggs. Different holiday.

252.
Answer: Jolly.

253.
Answer: Christmas coloring book.

254.
Answer: Since the snow is melted, it won't take any time at all.

255.
Answer: Mr. Scrooge.

256.
Answer: A heater.

257.
Answer: A melted snowman.

258.
Answer: I am Santa Claus and I am deciding who is naughty or nice.

Christmas Riddles

259.
Answer: Candy store.

260.
Answer: In a dictionary.

261.
Answer: The name of the town is Friday.

262.
Answer: Father Christmas.

263.
Answer: Forgiveness.

264.
Answer: Garland.

265.
Answer: Christmas scarf.

266.
Answer: The artificial one. The real one does not have to be assembled.

267.
Answer: Mike grabs two candy canes, but not from the tree.

268.
Answer: Ebenezer Scrooge.

269.
Answer: First snowfall.

270.
Answer: Only decorate the tree, since it is a tradition.

271.
Answer: Airport.

272.
Answer: The less fortunate.

273.
Answer: She gave just one to both of her friends to share.

274.
Answer: Five golden rings.

275.
Answer: Tommy is also a reindeer.

276.
Answer: He had no belly button.

277.
Answer: The trash can was right next to the elf's workstation.

278.
Answer: Why walk, when you can fly.

279.
Answer: Pinecone

280.
Answer: The nursery.

281.
Answer: There was a snowman there.

282.
Answer: He's trying to deck the halls.

Christmas Riddles

283.
Answer: Santa. He has the sleigh. We never said it was a foot race.

284.
Answer: His reindeers' vet, his elves' doctor and his sleigh's mechanic.

285.
Answer: Heat exhaustion.

286.
Answer: Snowball.

287.
Answer: Inflatable Santa Claus decoration.

288.
Answer: Clothing.

289.
Answer: I believe I can fly.

290.
Answer: They were able to track him with his phone.

291.
Answer: When he turned that other way. Otherwise, he kept making all of the RIGHT turns.

292.
Answer: The elves have no hiding spot in the South Pole.

293.
Answer: Because they are flying.

294.
Answer: Santa. He is playing with them today.

295.
Answer: He forgot to wear gloves.

296.
Answer: Pole numbers.

297.
Answer: Blitzen does not have a red nose.

298.
Answer: They will Fawn all over you.

299.
Answer: The grandma is also a mother. Her daughter is also a mother. Plus, there is her daughter. So, there are two mothers, two daughters and a grandma.

300.
Answer: He can eat them anytime, since it is Christmas morning.

301.
Answer: The person in the new office is Billy's mom.

One Final Thing…

Thank for making it through to the end of *Fun Christmas Riddles and Trick Questions for Kids and Family,* let's hope it was fun, challenging and able to provide you and your family with all of the entertainment you needed for this rainy day (or sunny afternoon)!

Did You Enjoy the Book?

If you did, please let us know by leaving a review on AMAZON. Review let Amazon know that we are creating quality material for children. Even a few words and ratings would go a long way. We would like to thank you in advance for your time.

If you have any comments, or suggestions for improvement for other books, we would love to hear from and you and can contact us at **riddleland@riddlelandforkids.com**

Your comments are greatly valued, and the book have already been revised and improved as a result of helpful suggestions from readers.